Flying with Wax Wings

Julie Koloini

BookLeaf Publishing

India | USA | UK

Flying with Wax Wings © 2024 Julie Koloini

All rights reserved.

No part of this publication may be reproduced, stored in a retrieval system, or transmitted, in any form or by any means, electronic, mechanical, photocopying, recording or otherwise, without the prior written permission of the presenters.

Julie Koloini asserts the moral right to be identified as author of this work.

Presentation by *BookLeaf Publishing*

Web: www.bookleafpub.com

E-mail: info@bookleafpub.com

ISBN: 9789363318281

First edition 2024

For My Parents

I Touched

I Touched

blue sapphires, blue torches,
a volt, the minotaur, truth.
He touched the sun, liberty,
was sure of the Serengeti for months.

Come, the icy breath of Lords,
in the past, delve into winter
and never see gardens or deserts,
grief or malcontent. Son, you

nearly touched the light overhead,
dove into death. Love
passed ugly into chiming
bells, primarily a veneer.

Son, I strapped speech,
truth, and solitude
to you and so, like a piano
you were interred.

Come, night, my son has fallen!
Profoundly and mysteriously
I touched the sky and clouds, giant
days hung of milled steel.

Icarus

Icarus, he caught the key.

Guard the marquee; I'll be incognito,
a friend, individually laced with my carnival
ring. Of course, a cheery sound sublime
may reduce some ornament of song.

Icarus, he caught the key.

Lastly, peal a bell brutally, sweetly,
After he desecrates the ceiling
He'll wander far looser tomorrow.

Could he even make sculptures of wings?

Impression of Ireland
(While Flying with Wax Wings)

He respires, has invented,
freed all oceans. Go free,
solid Pangea, cover mountains,
Pangea and lava - the face of the curious.

He almost traveled over
prairie, then blue prairie,
deep and very dense. He
chases, dissolves in air - transparent -
dies new, oil based. Accuse

ill silence, still lava.
Go truly and go tell truth,
a silence, air tempered,
all bearing color,
herbs and contaminated
croissants. He roars,
"The moon is nervous!"

Never tell a language ancient,
paroled from my labyrinth,
what's appropriate,
lordly, significant, primary.

Ache leaves mountains hanging
magically - named Remote,
Legendary, or Fionn Mac Cumhail -
insecure anchors of diamond and grain. He
traveled on incantations or more.

Chrysanthemum Garden

I want to plant a garden full
of Chrysanthemums –
Heady blooms swinging in the air
Like Goddesses rooted in the field –

But mostly just so I can sing
the word to myself as I till the soil;
toiling, the melody smoothly rolling
off my tongue:
Chry-san-the-mums.

The Impossible Pawn Shop Trick
(or, The Trick God is Playing on You)

I know a pawn shop guy who can send you back
  in time
and not just metaphorically, because in this
  poem

the pawn shop guy can do anything; so he sends
  you
back in time to 1970 with money to buy

artifacts – cheap – to sell as antiques for profit.
You see, this pawn shop guy confronted God

about the rumor that he and the Devil
were actually good friends, and that all of

Earth is part of an elaborate bet for one dollar
that has gotten completely out of hand

because neither God nor the Devil like to lose
a bet. Well, God had to keep the pawn shop guy
  quiet

somehow or he might blow the whole charade,
so he offered to let the pawn shop guy bend a
  few rules.

But you, back in 1970, run into two hundred
frat brothers all dressed in ruffled tuxedos, for
  some reason

and they rob you of your money, but they can't
  use
it because they are newly redesigned dollar bills

from 2004 that look like fake money from the
  future,
and we all know that time travel is impossible.

Enjoying an Antarctic Evening in Autumn

the night is an emperor penguin
its cummerbund too tight
his feathery middle squeezed
bursting over the top
with a melodious pop
filling the air with candy

futile flapping of wings tastes mute

icebergs crushed our *endurance*
shackleton didn't discover the south pole
he merely found it late
the stars were his map
twinkering in heaven
always too busy to rest

the formal flag of independence is faded

moonlight makes men rational
my penguin dances a jig for her
tomorrow night she will watch
as the stars learn a new routine
this ballet will be colder and
she must close her eyes to see

enjoying an antarctic evening in autumn

creo que dios
también es un pinguino
the penguin laughs at her
embarrassed
as the seams in his tuxedo burst

Shadow Angel

Everything can cast a shadow,
except an angel.
Angels are born in the clouds
like waves formed in the sea.

Shadows persist - black oxygen -
air exhaled from the mouths of angels.
I am only my mother's sweet
perfume, born first of my father.

I was born beautiful
and everyone wanted to touch me,
an angel whose shadow
disobeyed, looking for a fight.

There is a certain brevity in the light
which causes blindness
I un-name myself so that I can see in the dark,
scrutinize the edges of this weird summer:

Now we've reached the August
part, blazing and scorching
Tell the sun to give it up, and take
the pacing moonlight and midnights with her.

But it was only in dreaming

We lived in an old house with a basement
floor that could be lifted up
There was dirt underneath
So we dug with our bare hands
and found money. Damp bills, wrinkled
a bit, but money. And bones.
Angry bones.

The money belonged to the bones.

I dreamed I was having a nightmare
I couldn't wake from
I was screaming louder and louder
So you would wake me
But it was only in dreaming

Then the dream looped back

We were digging again
this time with shovels
I hit something hard with a clang
Resonating like a treasure chest
but I knew it was a coffin

Inside there was dirt, and three
ten dollar bills, and I thought,
that will never divide
evenly between us two
unless we make change.

The Day that Blackberry Jam Spilled

Don't tell me not to lick the blackberry
stains off the cathedral wall. I don't care
about Kentucky fireflies or a starling's song.

Back when the blade of your mezzaluna was still
sharp and clean, we would lie in the grass
make wishes on dandelions
and watch the clouds dissipate into thin air.

When you painted that statue of Mary
blue and the priest wasn't watching,
you kissed me and ran your sticky
fingers through my curly hair.

Don't you remember the day that blackberry jam
was spilled?

I am an envelope

I am an envelope

made of fine Japanese paper
and origami is a sunny sky
in the afternoon
when I pick Polly up

from work on the back
of my freshly painted paper crane
that smells of Earl Grey.
Her breath smells like my chocolate

ice cream tasted when Suki
and I went to the ice cream shoppe.
I wonder how she had time
to eat sweets at work.

I never have time
for dessert until I finish
washing the dishes. It's never sunny
when Suki and I fold paper.

Polly, put the kettle on, we'll all have tea,
in chipped mugs, spiced with cinnamon
that matches the red-gold curtains
above the sink. If the china wasn't chipped,

we wouldn't taste the cinnamon -
truth, according to Polly.
The paper airplane of truth circles overhead,
its motor running sleepily.

Polly drank a cup of milk and sugar
when she jumped from the plane,
and didn't spill a drop.
I watched her only halfway down the sky

because the sun was a blinding spot.
She says that silent films are coming back
with all their sad violins, secrets
and the sugary picture that always tells the truth.

Polly, Suki and I will all go to the theater
and watch the film with our eyes shut.
We'll bring our own snacks;
sneak hot tea in past the usher.

But the sugary picture is lying now
y los papeles no hacen ruido,
except the rough and rude sand paper
I'm using to make a crass paper crane,

since mine is watching a silent film
and drinking all our tea. Today
Polly will have to walk home from work,
across the freshly painted sun in the sky.

I dreamed I was a hot air balloon

I dreamed I was a hot air balloon
Glowing brightly in the night
Square blocks, rainbow pattern
But you were holding me down
Hard against the cold earth
You tied me down and staked me
But I didn't go down quietly
This isn't naptime
I struggled
I strained
I thrashed and I screamed
And I pulled at those ropes until I could feel
them tearing my skin
Hot air and blood gushing out
It doesn't matter
I won't be held down
I belong in the sky
I belong in the breeze
The wind is my home
The feral geese are my neighbors
And I will rest among the tree tops once more
I will rise
I will fly
Even if it kills me

I Grew Up in Texas

I grew up in Texas -
and I don't mean as a child

My childhood was Ohio and myths
and fairy pools and the Isle of Skye

I've never had enough imagination
but I always liked to imagine that I did

Devouring my previous lives like a fossilized fly
inside a fossilized lizard inside a fossilized snake

There was an old lady who swallowed a fly who
swallowed herself as a child

I am consumable
and potentially flammable
and probably a hazard to myself

Russian Doll Situation

when I was a child, I identified
with the smallest doll nestled
warm in the center, protected, special

and each other doll was separate
mother, grandmother, great grandmother
some ancestor so ancient as to be unimaginable

but imagine her I did
for there she was, undeniable
brown lacquered hair
red lips, rosy cheeks
blue dress and shawl

now I realize I am all the dolls

in the beginning, I was the younger
babe painted bright with heart
shaped flowers, next I grew
and the next doll clamped shut

a new persona obscured the old
daughter, student, friend, lover, mother
like a snake sheds its skin
but in reverse

I am growing new skins, building walls
putting on protective scales like armor

how many layers do I have now?
ugly, smelly layers like an onion
some will make you cry
if I take them apart at the seams
examine what's beneath, will I be able to
forgive?
can I put us back together into me?
how long can I play this game?

I am not hatching like a bird from an egg
I'm no phoenix, rising from the ashes
I'm not even sure I'm like a pearl
that forms from irritating, scratchy sand
still, I'm the largest doll yet

Fallen

we all slept here and it was a mistake
a sin, an infestation
it started small and unseen
unclean and unholy

we bathe in the ocean
see the sand up close
heaving with tiny life
full of broken bits, jagged

I feel like a leper washing
in the river we hide our shame
sun shining through a lace parasol
we wait and wait in vain

Where is Jesus? Forgiveness?
The Age of Miracles has ended
water will no longer turn to merlot

we are Untouchable now
we ask the Shaman for help
he gives us bones
piles them up and we wait like dogs

there is a wide circle of blood dripping
from the edges of the parasol
like from a crown of thorns
the blood is mine and yours both
now we are one

we go ask the Voodoo Queen for help
dark in her wood
she knows that we are twined
she gives us a needle and red thread
tells us to cut loose
then stitch ourselves back together

we are at war now with Vampires
the need, the lust, ever consuming
we set the bones and the thread and ourselves on
 fire
the heat will incinerate them all
along with our sins

Are we in Hell already?

When we were kids there were guns

When we were kids there were guns
We never really saw them
They were there just the same
Stashed in the washing machine
Hidden in a broken trash compactor

The sign on the door
one of the first things
I learned to read
"Trespassers will be shot
Survivors will be shot again"

He was at home alone, cleaning
a gun, shot a hole in the dresser
He always called it a bureau
Maybe he really was cleaning that gun
Maybe he flinched in the final second

A Baker's Dozen Reasons
Why

There was nothing interesting to do
She wanted to do it first
She wasn't looking for the brakes

She loved the shock factor
She hit the ground with her arms wide
Reckless abandon, wild tales

She would have loved to travel the world
But he didn't like to leave the house
Matching his and hers orange floral recliners

She would have to do it anyway
Never one to put things off

She ate the same white bread for 53 years

Rolling from the top of a hill
Gathering speed until the bottom
They lived on that hill for 25 years

She was restless
He bought her a new house
New furniture wouldn't cure her

She dumped the entire rack of freshly washed
  dishes on the floor
He bought new ones
Yellow with flowers on the edge

The boredom seeped in her marrow
a disease
they said it was staph in her blood

She loved attention, so we had her funeral three
  times
with purple roses, and then we buried her

She died because she was bored

Sleeping Deep

In the beginning
there was darkness
that stretched
uninterrupted
for leagues and leagues between
us, Mars and Earth

And then there was sleep
that sweet nothing
to help calm fears
of this darkness
and to help time pass
quickly, quietly

But mostly for protection
from heavy doses of radiation
that would burn away
our bodies like marshmallows
over a flame at night

At first the glow of hot
pink sugar is lovely
until there is nothing
but bitter black tar

And so, for these reasons
this crew slept and slept
heavy in dreaming pods
racing across the system
as if they were the only ones
on a Texas highway at night

Because of course they were
the only ones
this space is empty
a vacuum that sucks
up dreams

Rapture Bound

my mother is waiting for the end
the rapture was coming
leaving this life is bliss
Was I a bad kid?

my life, already over
the end written in Revelations
it sounds like trumpeting angels
it smells like horsemen and leather

Why should I go to school?
Get married and have kids?
the end is always nigh
it's fingers creeping up my spine

Yitzhak Yitzhak Rabin Rabin
Did the assassin have a choice?
written in a bible code
two thousand years ago

Can I find my name, Mommy?
no, it's only revealed to us after
like a charlatan's accidental trick
hindsight is a fool's best friend

the world was supposed to end
on my twelfth birthday
the rapture of October
we would fall like the orange leaves

Can you imagine my party?
interrupting the cake
pools of candle wax left behind
the rapture is hard to schedule

like dry cleaners working strictly business hours
you can't clean your suit while you wear it
inaccessible forgiveness
clean the stain from the wool

sheep sheep bleating for respite
credit card debt you still have to pay
twenty two years later strains
your credibility and this rapture affair

Forgive me. I cannot stand
to discuss any year that ends in 777
the flaming sword of the lord swinging
across the barren earth greedy men destroyed

but I am still living
the only way I can go on
jaded - but I love this life
the world is not ending

I am not interested
in the little black book of the antichrist
he never rsvp'd for this party
and he's not interested in your rapture either

At the End of the World, I Heard a Man Laughing

He laughed so hard
that the computer crashed

He laughed so hard
that the gun fired

He laughed so hard
that we all cried
his mother wept until her tears ran dry

He laughed until
the icebergs melted
the seas rose
those coastal cities crumbled into the waves

He laughed
and democracy failed

He thought he would laugh
all the way to the bank

Grounded

dreams crashed in dirt
angels dashed out of heaven
raining flaming feathers
ripped right from wings

wrong
it's all wrong

grounded

in red dirt
like my blood
like my hair
like my soul

Now I feel at home in the red clay places
soothing something inside me
wash that old stardust off my hands
scrub beneath my nails

Don't Scoff at the Moon

Oh My God! Look at the Moon!
don't scoff at the Queen of the Sky
feel the pull of the tides
shedding my former self
lights beaming from somewhere inside

the summer solstice and the strawberry moon
making wine
the sun wears her emotions bravely
everyone watching her fury flying across the sky
her heartbreak dipping below the horizon

holding my vanity in your hands
what's my excuse?
I'm in competition with the moon
smug in the sky
for the pull of your eyes